D0443289

This little book
belongs to

For Mother O' Mine

by
Mary Engelbreit

Andrews and McMeel
A Universal Press Syndicate Company
Kansas City

10 9 8 7 6

ISBN: 0-8362-4605-5

Library of Congress Catalog Card Number: 91-78253

For Mother O' Mine

Where there is home,
there's a mother who cares...

HOME

IS WHERE ONE STARTS FROM

T.S. ELIOT

who gives comfort...

THE COMFORTER

and kindness...

...who listens and shares.

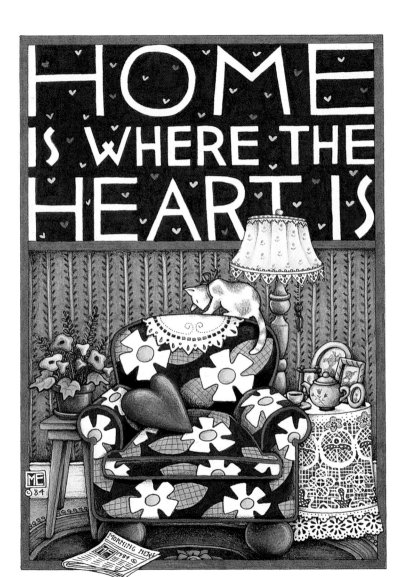

Every Mother is a

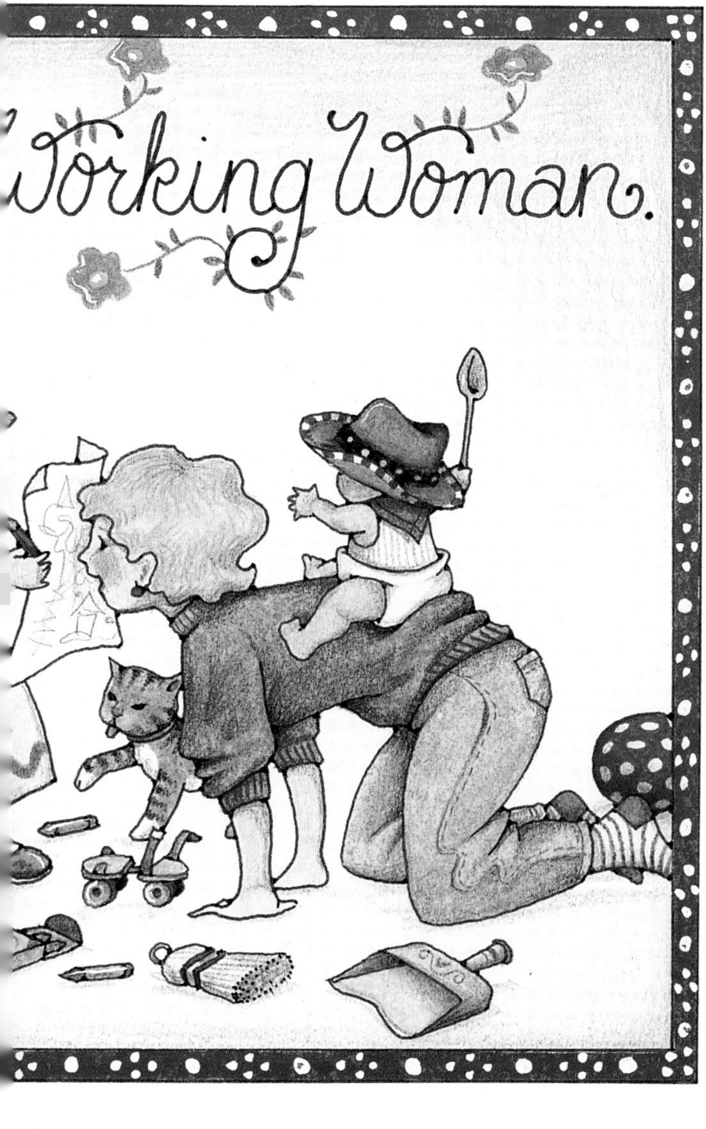
Working Woman.

Where there is home
there's a mother who sees

MY HOME IS IN MY MOTHER'S EYES.

we need good times…

...and laughter,
and sometimes a squeeze.

BE WARM, IN

Where there is home
there are children who know

IT'S GOOD TO
BE QUEEN

that they may need a push...

THANKS for

The PUSH!

...if they're ever to grow.

There are children who feel
that they're never alone...
for wherever a mother's love goes,
there is home.

THERE IS ALWAYS ONE MOMENT IN CHILDHOOD WHEN THE DOOR OPENS AND LETS THE FUTURE IN.

— GRAHAM GREENE